tiger pups

By TOM and Allie Harvey with Sarah L. Thomson

Photographs by TOM Harvey · Additional photographs by Keith Philpott

Collins

An Imprint of HarperCollinsPublishers

Foreword

As a father, it has been my great privilege to coauthor half a dozen books for children with my young daughters, Isabella and Juliana. These true stories about remarkable animals (including the immensely popular *Owen & Mzee*) have taken us on extraordinary journeys across three continents.

When I saw the first pictures of a golden retriever nursing three adorable white tiger cubs abandoned by their mother at a zoo in Kansas, I was intrigued. Then I learned that the golden retriever's name was Isabella (also the name of my younger daughter) and that two other retrievers, Sammy and Sonny, were helping Isabella raise the cubs.

We are a family of golden retriever lovers, with two of our own. In the past we had two other dogs also named—quite eerily—Sammy (also a golden) and Sonny (a frisky border collie). So there you have it: two sets of characters identically named Isabella, Sammy, and Sonny somehow connecting us by sheer coincidence or perhaps fate.

For the three of us, this was an important story, one about much more than just learning to get along. About ten years ago, President Clinton's cat, Sox, and dog, Buddy, became media darlings, famous for fighting with each other. Juliana, then three, was fascinated by their pugnacious relationship. She wanted President Clinton to tell Sox and Buddy that "they didn't have to like each other, but they did have to learn how to get along." When I shared Juliana's tip personally with the president, he laughed and said perhaps that message should become part of our foreign policy.

When I first spoke to Tom and Allie Harvey, we quickly established a common bond. When they brought their Isabella, Sammy, and the tiger cubs to New York to appear on NBC's *Today* show, Juliana, my Isabella, and I had the chance to spend time with all of them. It was quite obvious that these dogs and tiger cubs had, on their own, trumped Juliana's advice to President Clinton. Not only had they learned to get along, but they also very clearly and genuinely liked each other. As we learned from the unusual friendship between Owen and Mzee, a hippo and a giant tortoise, anything is possible! Here is Tom and Allie's wonderful story about the animal world's newest diplomats, who created a truce between the cats and dogs—and saved three lives. A truly valuable lesson for all of us.

Craig Hatkoff

Juliana Hatkoff

Isabella Hatkoff

On July 27, 2008, three white tiger cubs are born.

Each tiny cub is about the size of a guinea pig. They cannot see or walk. They call for their mother in high-pitched squalls. But after nursing the cubs for one night, their mother leaves them alone. They cry for her, but she does not come back.

The three tiger cubs were not born in India or China or Russia or any of the places where tigers live in the wild. They were born in Kansas, inside a wildlife park. Tom and Allie Harvey, who own the park, see that the cubs' mother, Sassy, is not taking care of them. They don't know why, but they know the babies need help. Tom and Allie bring the cubs into their own house.

Newborn tiger cubs need a *lot* of care. They need to be fed every two hours. They need to be washed and cuddled and kept dry and warm.

Luckily, Tom and Allie have someone to help.

Her name is Isabella.

Tom, Allie, Isabella (center), Sonny (bottom: left), and Sadie the puppy (center: right; bottom: center) play with the tiger pups.

This is Isabella.

A month before the three tiger cubs were born,

Isabella gave birth to puppies.

Her puppies are now old enough to eat solid food.

And the tiger cubs need milk.

Tom and Allie bring the cubs to Isabella.

She sniffs them and licks them.

She lets them nurse

just as if they were her own puppies.

Now they are tiger pups!

The tiger pups are tiny and weak.

They do not open their eyes.

They eat and sleep.

And they grow and grow and grow.

When the tiger pups are big enough
to drink from bottles,
Tom and Allie can feed them too.
Everyone is busy trying to keep
three hungry tiger pups fed!

Soon the tigers are seven weeks old.

They are about the size of small dogs.

Their bright blue eyes are open.

They still eat and sleep a lot,

but now they do more.

They climb. They run.

They nibble on everything!

They are trying to find out all they can

about their world.

Nasira is bold.

She loves to explore.

She stalks and pounces on her sisters.

Anjika likes to cuddle.

Sidani seems shy.

She spends time alone

or stays close to Allie.

The tigers keep playing
and sleeping and growing.
Now they are old enough to try eating meat.
They still cuddle and nurse with Isabella too.

If a tiger pup seems scared,

Allie holds her close. She makes a sound

called a chuffle by blowing air through her teeth.

This is what tigers say to each other.

The tiger pups feel safe when they hear this sound.

It means someone is taking care of them.

The tiger pups discover the world outdoors.

They are curious about the grass.

What is it? Will it hurt them?

Soon they get used to it.

Grass is good for tiger games—

hiding and stalking and chasing.

Tiger pups love indoor games too.

They tug and pull.

They pounce and wrestle and roll.

They bite, but not hard enough to hurt.

The tiger pups play with each other.
They play with a big blue ball.
They play with Tom and Allie
and with Isabella and Sadie,
one of Isabella's puppies.
Playing makes them strong.
It teaches them how to be tigers.

After playtime comes bath time.

Wild tigers love to swim in ponds or pools.

But baths are different!

The tiger pups put their ears back

and try to scratch.

They make high-pitched cries.

But soon they're warm and dry again.

When tiger pups are worn out,
they fall asleep anywhere—
on laps, on the floor, on couches, or on Isabella.
When they wake up, they're hungry again.
It's time for meat from bowls
or milk from bottles.

All three tiger pups spend more time outside.

Tom and Allie teach them to walk on a leash.

At first they don't like it.

They shake their heads and growl.

But they need to learn.

After the pups practice with the leash,

Tom and Allie let them run free.

Now the tiger pups are eleven weeks old.

They're too big to stay inside Tom and Allie's house.

It's time for them to move outdoors.

Nasira and Anjika and Sidani will grow up.

But they will remember Isabella

and Tom and Allie and all the people

who took care of them when they were tiger pups.

This book is dedicated to our "zoo" family.
You know who you are and that we love you!

ACKNOWLEDGMENTS

We would like to acknowledge the countless number of people who over the years have shared the dream of Safari Zoological Park with us and our family—human and furry.

Our vision for the park was born out of love for animals but has been kept alive by all the people who have sustained the zoo over these past twenty years with prayers, hard work, time, and financial support. We gratefully acknowledge all you have done: working with us, crying with us, laughing with us, praying with us, and supporting us. We would like to give a special thank-you to Oma and T. L. Harvey for their dedication and love for the people who have visited the park and for their service to the animals. Lastly, we acknowledge the one true supreme being, God our creator and Jesus Christ our savior, without whom we would be nothing. "In His hand is the life of every creature and the breath of all mankind." (Job 2:10)

PARK INFORMATION

Tom and Allie Harvey live outside Caney, Kansas, on the grounds of their zoo, Safari Zoological Park. The park has been in operation since 1989 and is dedicated to education, propagation, and conservation of endangered species. Safari Park is home to a variety of big cats—lions, tigers, serval, mountain lion, and spotted leopards—as well as grizzly and black bears, baboons, macaques, lemurs, coatimundies, and wolves. The Harveys belong to the Feline Conservation Federation, which promotes the conservation of all endangered wildcats.

Title page; p. 3; p. 5, top row: left, center; middle row; bottom row; pp. 6-14; pp. 16-17; p. 22, bottom; p. 27, bottom; p. 28, bottom; p. 31, photographs copyright © 2009 by Tom Harvey

p. 2; p. 4; p. 5: top row, right; pp. 15, 18-21; p. 22, top; pp. 23-26; p. 27, top; p. 28, top; pp. 29-30, p. 32, photographs © 2009 by Keith Philpott